DINOSAURS

 E**X**TREME FACTS

BY JOHN WOOD

©2019
The Secret Book
Company
King's Lynn
Norfolk PE30 4LS

ISBN: 978-1-912502-38-7

Written by:
John Wood
Edited by:
Madeline Tyler
Designed by:
Jasmine Pointer

A catalogue record for this book
is available from the British Library.

PHOTO CREDITS

CONTENTS

Words that look like <u>this</u> can be found in the glossary on page 24.

DINOSAURS

A long time ago, the world used to be ruled by reptiles of all sorts of shapes and sizes. They were called dinosaurs.

Dinosaurs lived on Earth from around 235–66 million years ago.

Dinosaurs lived on land, and walked on two, or four legs.

This means flying dinosaurs, like Pterodactyls, were not actually dinosaurs.

Around 700 <u>species</u> of dinosaur have been found.

There were two types of dinosaur:
lizard-hipped and bird-hipped.

Lizard-Hipped

Bird-Hipped

Dinosaurs may have **had soft feathers,** a fuzzy kind of hair **called 'down',** or hard, scaly skin.

Scientists think that feathered or fuzzy dinosaurs looked bright and colourful.

5

BIG AND SMALL

Sauropods were giant, plant-eating dinosaurs, with long tails and necks. Brachiosaurus, Diplodocus and Apatosaurus were sauropods.

Sauropod

Young sauropods gained around 2,000 kilograms (kg) in weight every year.

The biggest dinosaur footprint measured 1.7 metres (m) long. That's almost as long as a person lying down.

A tiny dinosaur called Anchiornis weighed around 110 grams (g), and was only 30 centimetres (cm) tall.

37 m

The biggest dinosaur was Patagotitan mayorum. It was around 37 m long. That's longer than seven cars in a row.

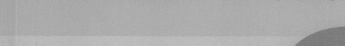

KG

Patagotitan was also the heaviest dinosaur, weighing around **69,000 kg.** An African elephant only weighs 6,000 kg.

Scientists think it might be **impossible** for a land animal to grow much bigger than Patagotitan mayorum did.

THE PLANT-EATERS

Most dinosaurs ate plants.
Plant-eaters are called herbivores.

Plant-eating sauropods ate 454 kg of plants every day. That's as heavy as a horse.

All the dinosaurs that walked on four legs were herbivores.

Plates

Stegosaurus may have had <u>blood vessels</u> in their plates. When angry, the plates would turn pink to warn other dinosaurs to stay away.

Instead of chewing, some **herbivores may have** swallowed stones to crush the plants in their stomach.

Some plant-eaters, like Hadrosaurus, had up to 1,000 teeth!

Pachycephalosaur's skull was 25 cm thick. It used its skull as a weapon.

Ankylosaurs had thick armour on their backs and heads. Some even had armoured eyelids.

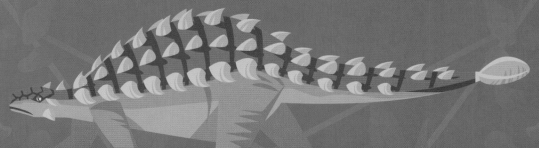

THE MEAT-EATERS

Some dinosaurs ate other animals.
Meat-eating animals are called carnivores.

Spinosaurus was the largest carnivore. It would also swim to catch <u>prey</u>.

Coelophysis was probably the fastest dinosaur. It could run 48 kilometres per hour (kph).

Velociraptors were about 90 cm tall and had feathers.

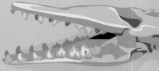

Meat-eating **dinosaurs** walked on two legs.

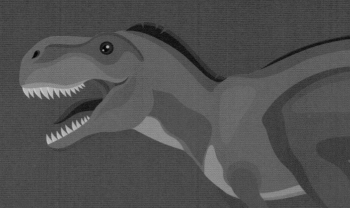

When the meat-eating Limusaurus grew up, it lost its teeth and became a toothless herbivore.

Tyrannosaurus rex could eat up to 230 kg of meat in one bite.

Tyrannosaurus rex had the most powerful bite of any dinosaur – more than twice as powerful as the biggest living crocodiles today.

LIFE AS A DINOSAUR

Some dinosaurs would travel in a herd.
There could be around 20 dinosaurs in a herd.

Some herds were a mix of different dinosaurs.

Stegosaurus was not very clever.
Although this dinosaur was nine metres
long, its brain was the size of a lime.

All dinosaurs laid eggs.

**Dinosaurs made nests for their eggs.
Most dinosaurs covered their nest, probably with plants, while some kept their nests open.**

Some dinosaurs, like sauropods, laid up to 30 or 40 eggs at a time.

**Some dinosaurs were good parents –
they cared for their <u>young</u> after they hatched.**

WHAT DID THE WORLD LOOK LIKE?

Dinosaur fossils (see page 20) have been found on every <u>continent</u> in the world.

Some plant-eating dinosaurs, especially sauropods, may have travelled around 300 km every year in search of food and water.

Millions of years ago, the continents were different shapes and closer together.

Eurasia

North America

South America

Africa

India

Antarctica

Australia

The world was much warmer. There were even lush forests in Antarctica.

14

Flowers only became wide-spread at the end of the Dinosaur time. Herbivores mostly ate ferns and conifers.

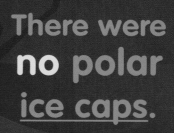

There were **no polar ice caps**.

Dinosaurs shared the world with other reptiles, giant insects and mammals.

The sea level was very high. Some parts of the world (like those which would become Midwest US and southern England) were underwater.

A LONG TIME AGO

Humans have only been around for 200,000 years.

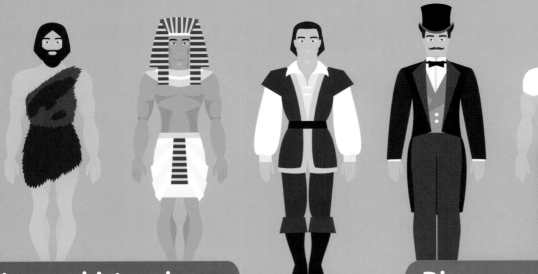

Human history has only been recorded for 5,000 years.

Dinosaurs ruled the Earth for over 160 million years.

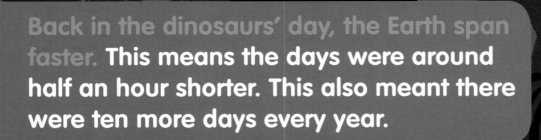

Back in the dinosaurs' day, the Earth span faster. This means the days were around half an hour shorter. This also meant there were ten more days every year.

Dinosaurs lived in three different times, or periods. Different dinosaurs lived in different periods.

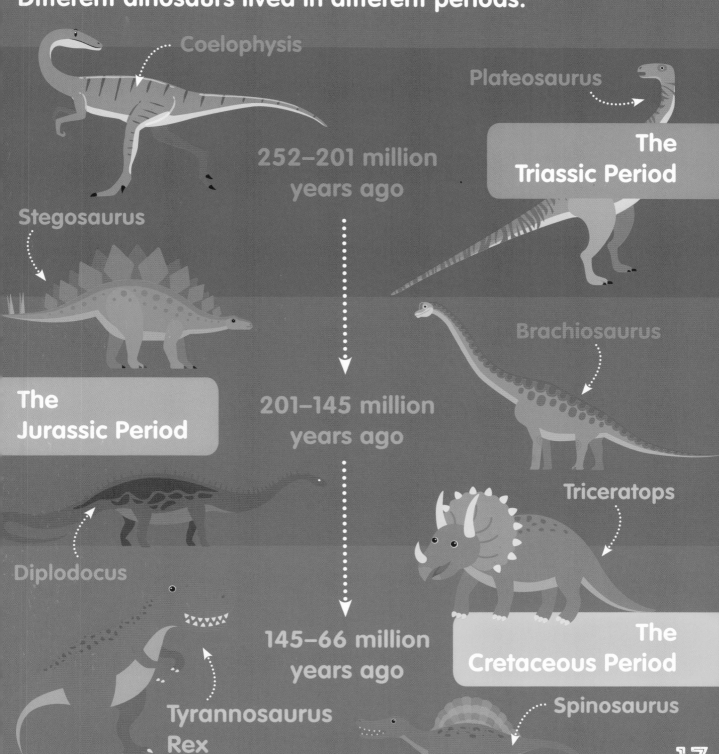

Coelophysis

Plateosaurus

The Triassic Period

252–201 million years ago

Stegosaurus

The Jurassic Period

201–145 million years ago

Brachiosaurus

Diplodocus

Triceratops

145–66 million years ago

The Cretaceous Period

Tyrannosaurus Rex

Spinosaurus

17

EXTINCTION

Dinosaurs went <u>extinct</u> around 66 million years ago. There are many ideas that explain why this happened.

Lots of **volcano eruptions might** have caused the <u>climate</u> to change.

Deadly diseases could have killed the dinosaurs. These diseases would have been carried by tiny insects.

However, most scientists think a giant <u>meteorite</u> hit Earth, killing all dinosaurs.

The meteorite would have been around 9 km wide.

The birds that are all around us <u>evolved</u> from dinosaurs.

However, it was the lizard-hipped dinosaurs that evolved into birds.
How confusing!

FOSSILS

Sometimes animals leave traces of themselves in rocks. This is called a fossil.

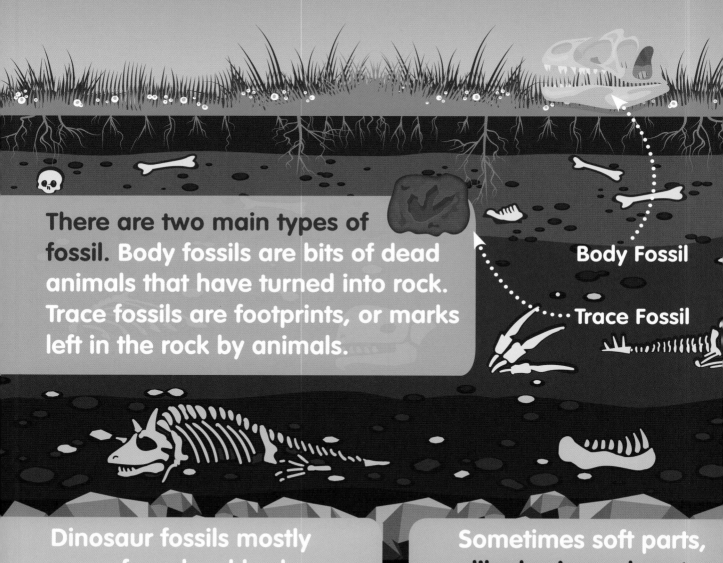

There are two main types of fossil. Body fossils are bits of dead animals that have turned into rock. Trace fossils are footprints, or marks left in the rock by animals.

Body Fossil

Trace Fossil

Dinosaur fossils mostly come from hard body parts, like teeth and bones.

Sometimes soft parts, like brains or hearts, can become a fossil too.

Fossils can also come from **poo**.

Everything we know about dinosaurs comes from fossils that are millions of years old.

Many dinosaurs had **hollow bones, like birds.**

Hollow bones were lighter because there was lots of empty space inside their bodies. This made it easier to move around.

PALAEONTOLOGISTS

A person who studies dinosaur fossils is called a palaeontologist.

Palaeontologists use all sorts of tools to find fossils, like shovels, pickaxes and even dynamite.

Dynamite

Pickaxe

Shovel

Some of the first dinosaur bones were found in China, between 265 and 316 AD. People believed that they were dragon teeth.

Egg Mountain is the name of a famous fossil site in Montana, US. Many fossils of nests and bones were found there, which told palaeontologists how dinosaurs lived.

One of the biggest dinosaur fossil sites is near Zhucheng city, China. Around 7,600 fossils have been found there.

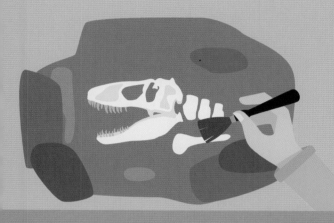

Anyone can be a fossil-finder. Mary Anning, who was not a trained scientist, found many fossils by the sea in the 1800s.

Othniel Marsh named more dinosaurs than anyone else...

...so far. Who knows what palaeontologists will find in the future?

GLOSSARY

blood vessels   tubes in the body through which blood flows

climate   the common weather in a certain place

continent   a very large area of land that is made up of many countries, like Africa and Europe

evolved   developed over a long time to become adapted to a certain habitat

extinct   when a species of animal is no longer alive

ice caps   sheets of ice that cover the most northern and most southern parts of the world

mammals   an animal that has warm blood, a backbone and produces milk

meteorite   a piece of rock that enters a planet's atmosphere without being destroyed

prey   animals that are hunted by other animals for food

species   a group of very similar animals or plants that are capable of producing young together

young   an animal's offspring or babies

INDEX